LOOPED

Matthew Lombardo

BROADWAY PLAY PUBLISHING INC
New York
www.broadwayplaypublishing.com
info@broadwayplaypublishing.com

Excerpts from *A Streetcar Named Desire* by Tennessee Williams used by permission of the University of the South, Sewanee, Tennessee.

Cover design: Fraver; photography: Walter McBride

First edition: May 2018
I S B N: 978-0-88145-765-0

Book design: Marie Donovan
Page make-up: Adobe InDesign
Typeface: Palatino

LOOPED was originally produced at the Lyceum Theatre in New York City by Tony Cacciotti, Chase Mishkin, Bard Theatricals, Lauren Class Schneider, Lawrence S Toppall and Leonard Soloway; Associate Producers: Barbara Freitag and David Mirvish, opening on 19 February 2010. The cast and creative contributors were:

TALLULAH BANKHEAD............................... Valerie Harper
DANNY MILLER...Brian Hutchison
STEVE .... Michael Mulheren

Director... Rob Ruggiero
Set design ....Adrian W Jones
Lighting design .... Ken Billington
Costumes..William Ivey Long
Sound design..............Michael Hooker & Peter Fitzgerald
Wigs .... Charles LaPointe
Production stage manager .... Bess Marie Glorioso

CHARACTERS & SETTING

TALLULAH BANKHEAD, 63, *an actress mostly known for her outrageous behavior and raunchy wit. Her grand persona shields her increasing insecurities, for her career has been on the downswing for some time.*

DANNY MILLER, 38, *a film editor. Attractive and bookish, he is an uptight conservative with an awkward charm. He doesn't like to talk about himself for he has a well-kept secret.*

STEVE, 45, *a sound engineer. Seen mostly in silhouette, he is an overweight, blue collar union worker with monotone speech.*

Summer 1965

A recording studio

Los Angeles

AUTHOR'S NOTE

During the Summer of 1965, an inebriated Tallulah
Bankhead entered a Los Angeles recording studio in an
effort to re-record (or "loop") a few lines of dialogue
from her final film *Die, Die My Darling*.

After hearing the audio recording of that very session,
(and enjoying a fair amount of artistic license) I
introduce this play as a loosely based chronicle of that
very event and a tribute to one hell of an outrageous
life!

In Loving Memory
of
Valerie Harper

ACT ONE

(A recording studio in Los Angeles. Summer: 1965. 2 P M.)

(The set is monochrome in color, an earth-toned shell of a mostly vacant sound stage. In the center of the studio is a large rectangular platform. A small table is placed on the left side of the landing.)

(There is a telephone, a pitcher of water, a glass, and a box of tissue on the table. On the center of the riser stands a comfortable high-backed stool. Hanging three feet above the stool is a large microphone. On the opposite side of the platform is a sofa and small coffee table.)

(As the house lights dim, an uptempo instrumental version of "Paper Moon" can be heard.)

(As the lights come up, DANNY MILLER pokes his head into the room. Making certain no one is around, he eventually enters. He locates a sound reel on a nearby chair, picks it up and starts to leave. When he is almost out the door, STEVE is heard over the loudspeaker.)

STEVE: That ain't it.

DANNY: *(Startled)* Ohh. Steve. You scared me. I thought you'd be gone by now.

STEVE: You and me both.

DANNY: I just came in to pick up that Bankhead reel and get it over to edit.

STEVE: You got the wrong tape.

DANNY: Oh. Sorry. Did you already send it over? Because there was nothing in my office when I left a few minutes ago.

STEVE: That's because I didn't get it done.

DANNY: What do you mean you didn't get it done? Steve. All that's left to do on this picture is loop that one line. It was supposed to be finished this morning.

STEVE: And it would have been. If she was here. I'm still waiting for her to show up.

DANNY: Where's Narizzano? What does he have to say about all this?

STEVE: He had a few choice words. Then left. Got tired of waiting.

DANNY: Did he say where he was going?

STEVE: He mentioned something about—Barcelona.

DANNY: Look. Someone has got to get this done. Now. We're already way over-budget in this department and Mansky's not spending one more dime on this film after today. He's been on the warpath ever since he saw the dailies.

STEVE: I know. He sounded really pissed off when he called.

DANNY: Wait. What? Did you talk to him??

STEVE: That's how I know he called.

DANNY: What did he say?

STEVE: That you need to take care of this.

DANNY: Me? Oh-no. No-no. No. That's not my job. I am the film editor. And the definition of a film editor (according to my contract) is someone who (surprise) edits film. I don't record sound. That would be the sound editor. I don't deal with talent. That would be the director. I. Edit. Film. (*Beat*) Alone.

STEVE: Well, the director is boarding a plane and the sound editor just gave his notice.

DANNY: But I can't stay. Not today. Steve. Please. Look. You gotta call Mansky back and tell him I can't do this.

STEVE: I ain't playing monkey in the middle between you and Mansky. You want to bail? You call Mansky. Until then? You're in charge, Miller.

(Beat)

DANNY: *(Accepting)* Alright. Fine. I'm in charge. Great. So. Think-think-think. She's not here. And. *(A sudden idea)* I know. Maybe we can get a cover.

STEVE: A what?

DANNY: A stand-in. You know. A voice double who can record the line. Someone who sounds like Bankhead.

STEVE: There's always that sea lion at the aquarium.

DANNY: That is not funny. You are not a funny man. Come on now Steve. Will you help me find a way to get out of this?

STEVE: I would just cut the damn line.

DANNY: We can't do that.

STEVE: Why not?

DANNY: It's a plot point. That line is an integral part of the story. We need to know she's been banished from the church.

STEVE: She should have been banished from making this film.

DANNY: *(Thinking to himself)* Alright. So. We can't *cover* the line and we can't *cut* it. *(Gasps)* But we can *save* it!

STEVE: Uhh. No.

DANNY: Sure we can.

STEVE: We really can't.

DANNY: Just let me hear it.

STEVE: Miller.

DANNY: Play me the tape.

STEVE: Why?

DANNY: Maybe we can salvage it. You know. Clean up the track a little.

STEVE: Alright. Hold on.

(Beep. Beep. Beep)

TALLULAH: *(V/O)* And so Patricia— *(The sound of leaves crunching, bushes rustling and twigs snapping make the rest of the line comically impossible to hear)*

(Long pause. Then:)

DANNY: I hate this film. I have been putting in so much overtime on this damn picture and it is still completely unwatchable. Last week? The studio execs even changed the title: It's now called *Die, Die, My Darling*. They think it will sell more tickets.

STEVE: To who? Serial killers?

DANNY: Again. Not funny. Steve. Come on. This is serious. I can't hang around here today. I have to leave for the airport in an hour.

STEVE: I don't know what to tell you, man.

DANNY: What are we going to do if she doesn't show up?

(A 63 year old TALLULAH BANKHEAD immediately bursts into the room in a grandly disheveled manner. She is wearing a fur, a pair of sunglasses and carries an oversized handbag. Her inebriated strut is somewhat unsteady. Her speech, garbled.)

TALLULAH: Fuck Los Angeles. Hate it here. Always have. With the freeways leading into more freeways. And the street signs that aren't even in fucking English. *Sepulveda* this. *La Cienga* that. You have to be bi-lingual just to cross the goddamn street. The only good thing about L.A.? It's six hours from New York. Now New York: *That* is a great city. And you want to know why it's a great city? Because it was built for FUCKING MORONS. *Everything is numbered.* If you get lost in Manhattan? You don't *deserve* to be found. But the only place (and I do mean the only place) I truly love is London. And you want to know why I love London? Because they love ME in London! Every time I played the West End the show would be sold out *months* in advance. But that's not what I'm trying to say. No. Not what I'm trying to say at all. Because my point is—I mean, the point in ALL of life *really* is... *(Sees* DANNY*)* who the fuck are you?

DANNY: Miss Bankhead? I'm Danny. Danny Miller. I'm the film editor on this project. Looks like you're working with *me* this afternoon.

TALLULAH: Where's Silvio?

DANNY: Mr Narizzano had to leave unexpectedly.

TALLULAH: *(Pissed)* Leave?? Well, that's just shocking. What a shocking thing to do!

*(*TALLULAH *darts for the door.* DANNY *stops her.)*

DANNY: No-no-no. Miss Bankhead. Wait.

TALLULAH: The director should be here!

DANNY: I know. And it's a shame he couldn't stay. But not to worry. You can trust me.

TALLULAH: Really. Well. The last time a man said that to me I was standing on a diving board wearing nothing but a string of pearls.

DANNY: Why were you doing that?

TALLULAH: To prove I was a natural ash blonde.

DANNY: *(Uneasy)* Umm. Miss Bankhead. How would you like to start?

TALLULAH: I'd like to start by you cutting the Miss Bankhead crap is how I'd like to start. If you want to speak to a Miss Bankhead? Speak to my sister Eugenia. Course it's hard for her to have a conversation these days seeing that her head is so terribly far up her ass. And I'm so shamefully sorry to be late. But I got a tad lost. You see, I woke up bright and early this afternoon. The sun was shining. The birds were singing. My pharmacist delivered. So I say to myself: "Self? Take the goddamn Bentley out for a spin". See, I haven't driven that car in *ages* and thought it might be a hoot to cruise about town. Not to say I was on any particular prowl, mind you. But I simply *worship* that car and— and—what was I saying?

DANNY: You got lost.

TALLULAH: Yes. Right. Lost. So. I'm driving around this wasteland you people call a city. Didn't know where the fuck I was. So I stop at a phone booth. Call a cab. Get picked up and delivered here.

DANNY: So, where is the Bentley?

TALLULAH: Considering the one-block taxi ride? Apparently right across the street.

(TALLULAH *takes off her fur, tossing it to* DANNY.)

TALLULAH: And uuughh! It's bloody sweltering outside.

DANNY: Los Angeles in August usually gets that way.

TALLULAH: Had I known it was going to be this hot? I would have worn my other fur.

DANNY: Look. I am in a bit of a rush this afternoon. So if you don't mind I'd really like to get down to work.

TALLULAH: Yes. Right. Work. Splendid!

DANNY: Now I know you've done this many times before. So I don't need to explain how it all works.

TALLULAH: Actually dahling, I haven't made a picture in twenty years. So you might want to refresh my memory.

DANNY: Oh. Um. Alright. Well. There's just this one line in the film that is inaudible. So we need to re-record it to picture. You see, the boom operator hit a shrub with the microphone.

TALLULAH: Then why not have him record the fucking line?

DANNY: Miss Bankhead…

(TALLULAH *growls at* DANNY.)

DANNY: *(Shaken)* Miss—umm—Tallulah…

TALLULAH: Much better, darling.

DANNY: Didn't your agent explain why you were coming here today?

TALLULAH: No.

DANNY: Why not?

TALLULAH: He's been dead for three years. *(Beat)* And bully for that cause I was ready to murder the bastard. Do you know how many jobs that sonofabitch cost me?

DANNY: Oh, I can't imagine anyone not wanting to hire you. Now. Why don't you sit right over here so we can get started.

(TALLULAH *sits in the chair.*)

DANNY: You see, it's really rather simple. First? You're going to hear three beeps.

TALLULAH: Three.

DANNY: And at the end of the third beep—

TALLULAH: Third beep.

DANNY: —you say the line—

TALLULAH: Say line.

DANNY: —while matching your lips—

TALLULAH: Match lips.

DANNY: —to the picture on the screen up there.

TALLULAH: Up there.

DANNY: Okay?

TALLULAH: Brilliant.

DANNY: Great. Now. The line is: *(He grabs a nearby script and slowly reads the line.)* "AND SO PATRICIA, AS I WAS TELLING YOU, THAT DELUDED RECTOR HAS IN LITERAL EFFECT CLOSED THE CHURCH TO ME."

TALLULAH: And so Patricia—blah-blah-blah—closed the church to me. Fine.

DANNY: *(Picking up the headset)* Let's try this with sync?

TALLULAH: Oh, dahling. I'd love one.

DANNY: Excuse me?

TALLULAH: You asked if I wanted a drink.

DANNY: No. I said "with sync". And I wasn't speaking to you.

(TALLULAH looks around the empty room.)

TALLULAH: We have an imaginary friend with us, do we?

DANNY: His name is Steve.

TALLULAH: Oh, and you've named him. How sweet. When I was a little girl I had an imaginary friend. She didn't like me all that much. I think that's why I'm so terribly insecure. I mean, being rejected by an actual living being is one thing. But when your imaginary friend doesn't want to play with you? That can be downright traumatizing

DANNY: *(Faux sympathizing)* I'm sure it can be. *(Then back to business)* Can we just try one please?

TALLULAH: Let's.

(Beep. Beep. Beep. Silence)

DANNY: Tallulah?

TALLULAH: Hmm?

DANNY: That was it.

TALLULAH: That was what?

DANNY: Your cue.

TALLULAH: My cue for what?

DANNY: *(As if talking to a child)* The line. After the third beep you say the line while matching your lips to the picture on the screen up there. Did you not hear the beeps?

TALLULAH: I don't remember.

DANNY: Alright. Umm. No problem. We'll just go again.

TALLULAH: Smashing.

(Beep. Beep. Beep)

TALLULAH: Oh, I definitely hear those beeps now.

DANNY: Good.

TALLULAH: Charming tone.

DANNY: Great.

TALLULAH: Divine clarity.

DANNY: Yes. But you need to say the line.

TALLULAH: Pardon?

DANNY: *(Almost in disbelief)* The line. At the end of the third beep you say the line. Remember?

TALLULAH: Oh. Shit. Yes. Sorry. Listen sugar. I'm afraid my mind is not what it used to be. Thoughts fly in and out of here all the time these days.

DANNY: With me as well. I mean, it is so hard to understand things sometimes. Especially with the kind of work we are doing here. Lines.

TALLULAH: Yes.

DANNY: Beeps.

TALLULAH: Yes.

DANNY: So how about I make this a little easier for you, huh? Suppose we come at this in a completely different way.

TALLULAH: Marvelous.

DANNY: How about I give you a tap?

TALLULAH: A what?

DANNY: A tap.

TALLULAH: A tap?

DANNY: Instead of the beeps.

TALLULAH: No more beeps?

DANNY: No more beeps. I'll tap you instead.

TALLULAH: Perfect.

DANNY: Great. That's great. Here we go now.

(Beep. Beep. Beep. DANNY taps TALLULAH's shoulder.)

TALLULAH: Yes, dahling, what is it?

DANNY: That was it.

TALLULAH: That was what?

DANNY: The tap.

TALLULAH: That was the tap?

DANNY: That was the tap.

TALLULAH: I thought you were trying to get my attention.

DANNY: No. That was the tap.

TALLULAH: But I still heard beeps.

DANNY: Then I gave you the tap.

TALLULAH: You said no more beeps.

DANNY: But I gave you the tap!

TALLULAH: Well, you are overwhelming my sensory system. And quite frankly, if I'm going to get poked by a stranger? I better damn well enjoy it!

DANNY: I didn't poke you.

TALLULAH: You most certainly did.

DANNY: It was a tap.

TALLULAH: A poke! It was a poke, I tell you. *And don't fight with me!!*

DANNY: Who's fighting?

TALLULAH: You are! And I won't stand for it. I don't like fighters. My sister Eugenia? She's a fighter. She's also a liar, a thief, a drug addict, and on occasion a lesbian. *(Beat)* But she's very good company.

DANNY: *(Attempting to make peace)* Can we please just try this again?

TALLULAH: Yes. But don't poke me this time.

DANNY: I didn't poke you. I tapped you.

TALLULAH: Well, whatever it was, I didn't care for it. And listen, dahling, you needn't be so blasé about things. Specificity is what is required in order for us to have a proper communication here. Why, when I created the role of Blanche in *A Streetcar Named Desire* on Broadway—

DANNY: You never created that role on Broadway.

TALLULAH: I beg your pardon?

DANNY: I said…you never did *Streetcar* on Broadway.

(TALLULAH *feels* DANNY *knows something.*)

TALLULAH: *(Caught/covering)* Broadway? Oh. My mind. Did I say Broadway? No. I was thinking of London.

DANNY: *(One up on her)* Really? You played *Streetcar* in the West End?

TALLULAH: Well. Maybe not *exactly* there. But wherever it was—

DANNY: The Coconut Grove Playhouse. In Florida. Not Broadway. Not London. Flor-i-da. And I'm sure you must remember that production.

TALLULAH: *(Flippantly)* Yes. Well. Unfortunately I can't remember most of my life.

DANNY: How convenient for you. *(Making a point)* Or should I say "blasé"?

TALLULAH: I see you've done a little homework on me. Have you not?

DANNY: I am—*familiar* with some of your work.

TALLULAH: Then do tell, Mr Miller. I'm rather curious as to what you think of me?

DANNY: As an actress?

TALLULAH: *(Seductively)* As a woman.

DANNY: Is there a difference?

TALLULAH: You know, there are two kinds of men I encounter in life. Those who want to fuck me and those who want to *be* me. Into which category do you fall?

DANNY: *(Beat)* That would be neither.

(Beep. Beep. Beep)

TALLULAH: I'm sorry. I forgot the line, dahling.

DANNY: And *I'm* sorry but my name is Danny. You asked me to call you Tallulah? I call you Tallulah. Well, I would like to be called Danny.

TALLULAH: But all my life I've been terrible at remembering names. I was at a party once and introduced a friend of mine as "Martini". Her name was actually "Olive".

DANNY: Well, my name is Danny. D-A-N-N-Y. Danny. Not Olive. Not Martini. And especially not *"dahling"*.

TALLULAH: There's certainly no need to get your skirt in a twirl. From now on Tallulah will call you *Danny*.

DANNY: Thank you. Now—the line is: "AND SO PATRICIA, AS I WAS TELLING YOU, THAT DELUDED RECTOR HAS IN LITERAL EFFECT CLOSED THE CHURCH TO ME."

TALLULAH: And so Patricia—blah-blah-blah—closed the church to me. Fine.

(Beep. Beep. Beep)

TALLULAH: Where's my goddamn DRINK? Did I not order a DRINK!

DANNY: No. We went through this. You *thought* I said drink but I said *sync*. Remember?

TALLULAH: I still would very much like a cocktail. Because personally, I think it's terribly rude not to offer someone a drink when you invite them to your house.

DANNY: This isn't my house.

TALLULAH: Thank heaven for that. It's dreary as fuck in here. Now I'll take a bourbon and water. *(Beat)* Without water.

DANNY: Tallulah.

TALLULAH: You do have booze in this dump, do you not?

DANNY: I don't think it's a good idea that you drink during our recording session.

TALLULAH: I was drinking during the shoot. You want this shit to sound *authentic?!*

DANNY: Steve? We got any liquor up there?

TALLULAH: Ah. Your invisible friend drinks too? I like him already.

STEVE: Hold on.

TALLULAH: *(Spooked)* What the fuck was that?

DANNY: I told you. That's Steve. He's our sound engineer.

TALLULAH: You mean he's a real person?

DANNY: Yes.

TALLULAH: Ah. Answer to prayer! *(Flirtatiously)* Steve, dahling. Can you hear me?

STEVE: Yeah.

TALLULAH: Can you see me as well?

STEVE: Yeah.

TALLULAH: And do you not think I'm beautiful?

STEVE: Yeah.

TALLULAH: And beautiful women should *always* get what they want, isn't that right, Steve?

STEVE: Yeah.

TALLULAH: Well, this beautiful woman would very much like some bourbon. I'll make it worth your while, sailor.

STEVE: I don't sail.

TALLULAH: Oh, I can teach you. *Lots* of things. Secret things. Unspeakable things. *(She lifts her dress to mid-thigh.)* You know, I don't believe in undergarments —

(DANNY quickly intercedes by pulling TALLULAH's dress back down.)

DANNY: Dammit! Steve! Will you help me out here?!

TALLULAH: So sorry. I might have known you'd be allergic to fur.

STEVE: All we got is scotch.

TALLULAH: *(Exploding)* Scotch?? SCOTCH?! I never touch that poison! It's the devil's drink! Everyone knows Tallulah doesn't drink Scotch. If I were on a desert island dying of thirst I wouldn't drink that shit. I once gave my dog a sip of Scotch. He had to lick his ass just to get the taste out of his mouth! I swore (and I do mean swore) on my granddaddy's grave that Scotch would never EVER touch these lips!

DANNY: Well Scotch is all we got.

(Beat)

TALLULAH: Give me the bottle. Granddaddy will get over it.

(STEVE sticks his hand out of the projection booth.)

TALLULAH: Oh, dahling please be careful…the bottle.

(STEVE drops down a bottle of Scotch. DANNY catches it, gives the bottle to TALLULAH who carefully inspects the bottle's label.)

TALLULAH: Well liquor. I might have known. Cheap sons-of-bitches. I give you people forty years of my sweat and blood and all you can muster up is a half bottle of McCormick.

DANNY: You don't have to drink it.

TALLULAH: Of course I have to drink it. I'm an alcoholic for Christ's sake. That's what we DO. We DRINK. No matter how shabby the brand.

DANNY: So you *admit* you have a drinking problem?

TALLULAH: Of course I have a drinking problem. Whenever I'm not drinking? Oh honey, it's a problem.

DANNY: Clever. Very clever. But all kidding aside and whether you choose to acknowledge this or not— alcohol has a degenerative effect on the body.

TALLULAH: And don't I know it. When I drink? Ohhh. My poor legs.

DANNY: They swell?

TALLULAH: No. Open. *(She lights a cigarette.)*

DANNY: What are you doing now?

TALLULAH: You certainly can't expect me to drink and not smoke at the same time. What are you? Amish?! *(She grabs a glass off the table and pours herself a hefty cocktail. She downs it in one gulp. She pours herself another.)* Care to join me, Mr Miller?

DANNY: I don't drink while I'm working.

TALLULAH: And I don't work while I'm drinking. But *I've* made an exception.

(TALLULAH offers DANNY a glass.)

DANNY: I'm sorry. But I just think there is a time and a place for everything. And if I am to be totally honest here—I am finding your behavior and language this afternoon really inappropriate for a working environment.

(Beat)

TALLULAH: What the fuck are you talking about?

DANNY: See? That. Right there.

TALLULAH: Ohh dahling, please. Those are just words. I can say "shit" cause I'm a lady.

DANNY: Don't you think you should go easy?

TALLULAH: Dahling, I've gone easy my entire life. That's why I have so many penpals.

(DANNY *takes* TALLULAH'*s glass and puts it on the table.*)

DANNY: We really are short on time here. So can we please get going?

TALLULAH: Of course.

(Beep. Beep. Beep)

TALLULAH: *(With cigarette in mouth)* And so Patricia, as I was telling you —

STEVE: Cut.

DANNY: What?

STEVE: The cigarette.

TALLULAH: What about it?

STEVE: I need you to take it out of your mouth.

TALLULAH: You won't be saying that to me later.

DANNY: Tallulah please.

TALLULAH: But I just lit up.

DANNY: Doesn't matter.

TALLULAH: And it's my very last one.

DANNY: Please put it out now.

TALLULAH: But WHY?

DANNY: It's affecting your speech.

TALLULAH: No, dahling. The *liquor* is affecting my speech. The cigarette is calming my goddamn *nerves*.

DANNY: I'm just going to stand here until you put it out.

TALLULAH: *(Pouting)* Oh, Steve. How you've betrayed me. Now I'll only let you french-kiss me later. *(She takes the cigarette from her mouth and puts it out in a nearby ashtray, shooting* DANNY *a look.)*

DANNY: Thank you.

TALLULAH: Go to hell.

DANNY: *(Under his breath)* Already there.

(Beep. Beep. Beep)

TALLULAH: And so Patricia, as I was telling you —

(The phone rings.)

STEVE: Cut.

DANNY: Hold please. *(He crosses over to the phone, lifts the receiver.)* Recording. Studio B. *(…)* Ohh, she's still here. Yes. You can put it through. *(…)* Hello? What? Where? *Marrakesh??* *(…)* No! Absolutely not! Wait. Alright. Yes. Yes. I'll accept the charges. *(To Tallulah)* It's for you.

TALLULAH: Me?

DANNY: You.

TALLULAH: Who is it?

DANNY: I don't know.

TALLULAH: Well find out. I can't talk to a total stranger. Not in broad daylight anyway.

DANNY: *(Into phone)* May I ask who's calling please? *(To Tallulah)* It's your sister.

TALLULAH: Tell her I'm dead.

DANNY: That's not true.

TALLULAH: Then kill me so it will be.

DANNY: *(Back into phone)* Hello? Yes. I'm afraid Tallulah is unavailable at the moment but if you care to leave a— *(…)* Oh. Oh no.

TALLULAH: *(Under her breath)* Here we go—

DANNY: Oh. I'm so sorry. Wait. Yes. Let me see what I can do. *(To Tallulah)* She says she's in trouble.

TALLULAH: The Salem Witch Trials are over. She's safe.

DANNY: Will you *please* just take care of this??

TALLULAH: Oh, goddamn it! *(She grabs the receiver from DANNY.)*

TALLULAH: *(Into phone)* What the fuck do you want? And how did you get this number? *(...)* Cut to the chase, Sister. How much do you need this time? *(...)* Ten thousand dollars?? For what?! *(...)* Oh, you dizzy old cow. Didn't I tell you that boy would be nothing but trouble? And he's a drug dealer to boot! *(...)* "Good at what he does"?? He never has money and he never has drugs. *How good could he fucking be?! (In no mood)* Spare me the sugar act. You're giving me diabetes! *(...)* No. I am not coming out there. BUT. I will help you out because I am so terribly good-natured and it would be un-Christian, simply un-Christian of me to turn my back on blood—no matter how *polluted* that blood may be... *(...)* Just tell me where you're staying. Uhh-uhh. Uhh-uhh. Will you stop babbling I said I'd help. But this is it. This is the absolute last time! *(She slams down the receiver.)* How do I get an outside line?

DANNY: Dial nine.

(TALLULAH begins dialing.)

TALLULAH: Sister has always had an attitude problem. And I've never cared for women with attitude. Never. Joan Crawford was like that. She and her husband both. That revoooolting Fairbanks character. With whom I slept by the by. And I told Joan all about it. Right in front of him. We all were on a train once and I walked right up to Joan and said, "Dahling, I think you're divine. I also had an affair with your husband.

So you better watch out because you're going to be next". And she was. Oh, but Crawford was a lousy lay. She kept getting out of bed to beat the children. *(Then into phone)* Cal dahling. It's me. Listen baby. I need you to take ten grand out of the safe and get yourself on the next flight to Morocco. Tonight preferably. *(…)* Well, of *course* it's Sister. She's gone and got herself in a bit of a pinch with that drug lord she's been screwing and needs money to bail his ass out. *(…)* Oh, sweetie, you're a love. Call me when you get there. She's staying at La Lune (or in a nearby alley way when she's fucked up). *(…)* Yes. Alrighty then. Mmm-hmm. Mmm-hmm. Mmm-hmm. Bye-bye now, dahling. *(She hangs up the receiver.)* Christ only knows what they do together. The boy's twenty-two and Sister's older than the Red Sea. Oh, but who can blame her I suppose. Lord knows I do love sex.

DANNY: *(To himself)* Oh dear God—

TALLULAH: Although I must admit the conventional position makes me terribly claustrophobic. And the others? Well, I end up with either a stiff neck or lockjaw… Listen honey. This one time, a marine came up to me and said: "Tallulah, I want you in the worst way". "Well", I shot back. "The worst way I know is standing up in a hammock".

(TALLULAH laughs at herself, then realizes DANNY is not amused.)

DANNY: Is everything in life just a joke to you?

TALLULAH: Life *is* a joke, dahling. Well. For those of us who have a sense of humor.

DANNY: I happen to have a fine sense of humor.

TALLULAH: Are you planning to *unleash* it anytime soon?

DANNY: *(Turning serious, trying not to get angry)* You know, you're really not as entertaining as you might think. I mean, I'm sure it's fun to go through life with your pocketful of punch lines. All set to toss one out at any given time so people can comment on how witty you are. But some of us *don't* do that. Alright? Some of us *can't*. So can you please just respect that and let's get back to work?!

TALLULAH: Careful darling: We don't want people mistaking you for someone who actually has a pulse.

DANNY: I'm. Serious.

TALLULAH: Why are you in such a big hurry? Planning a little rendezvous later?

DANNY: Maybe. Yeah. Something like that. So what?

TALLULAH: Ahhh. An Affair to Remember. I do hope things work out a little better for you than they did for Deborah Kerr. Poor thing. Rushing to meet the love of her life and she ends up crippled.

DANNY: *(Somber)* Yeah. Well. Love is like that. Again please? *(He walks over and taps the stool.)*

TALLULAH: Alright. Alright. We must press on. Back to the salt mines. *(She crosses back to the platform and takes a seat.)*

(Beep. Beep. Beep)

TALLULAH: And so Patricia, as I was telling you—do you suppose we might take a teensy little break?

DANNY: You cannot be serious.

TALLULAH: I most certainly am. My union does allow for occasional rest. Of course to lay people such as yourself it's only an actor's union but still a union none the same. And considering my recent trauma with Sister and the fact that you've been working me like a hound, I'd very much welcome a break in these perfectly ghastly proceedings.

DANNY: *(Holding his tongue)* Ten minutes.

TALLULAH: Why, that's jolly decent of you.

DANNY: Steve?

STEVE: Yeah?

DANNY: Take ten.

STEVE: Right.

TALLULAH: Oh, Steve darling? You're more than welcome to join us.

STEVE: I'd rather just stay up here, where it's safe.

TALLULAH: *(To* DANNY*)* Not the most sociable of sorts, is he?

DANNY: But clearly very smart.

(The lights to the control booth go out as TALLULAH *empties the contents of her purse on the floor, searching through various paraphernalia.)*

TALLULAH: Just give me a moment to collect myself and then we'll get right back to—whatever the fuck we're doing here. *(She finds her "snuff box" of cocaine. She opens the lid, takes a spoonful with her pinky nail, snorts.)*

DANNY: What is *that??*

TALLULAH: Oh. Sorry. Here.

DANNY: No thank you.

TALLULAH: Ohh.

DANNY: Ohh what?

TALLULAH: Nothing.

DANNY: No, you just said "ohhh"—and I would like to know what you meant by that.

TALLULAH: Not important really. I just should have known you were one of those.

DANNY: One of whats?

TALLULAH: A goody-goody.

DANNY: *(Cryptically)* I'm hardly that.

(DANNY instinctively turns away from TALLULAH.)

TALLULAH: You're a tough one to figure out, Mr Miller. In fact, I'd venture to say that either you've never done a damn thing wrong in your entire life. Or. Perhaps. Just. Perhaps. You have a secret or two.

DANNY: Everyone has secrets.

(TALLULAH she studies DANNY.)

TALLULAH: You're a terribly unhappy young man.

DANNY: I am not *unhappy.*

TALLULAH: Then you must be Republican.

DANNY: *(Irritated)* Look. You don't know me. I don't know you.

TALLULAH: Yes. But the one thing I *do* know is pain when I see it. *(She snorts again.)*

DANNY: And you sure know how to relieve it.

TALLULAH: *(Indicates snuff box)* What? This? Ha!

DANNY: What you are doing is highly addictive.

TALLULAH: Cocaine? Addictive? Nonsense. I ought to know: I've been doing it for *years.*

(TALLULAH delights in DANNY's frustration as he sits in the corner and begins reading.)

TALLULAH: You're single, aren't you?

DANNY: I'm ignoring you.

TALLULAH: Just answer the question.

DANNY: Still ignoring you.

TALLULAH: Upp. Wait. I stand corrected. There's a ring on your finger.

DANNY: Not that it's any of your business but I happen to be a married man.

TALLULAH: Well that certainly explains your misery. And here I thought you were a bit of a queer.

DANNY: Well. I'm not.

TALLULAH: Oh, dahling, take no offense. Almost all the men I know are homosexuals (which perhaps explains why I can't get laid in this fucking town). People even think I swing that way as well. And I don't deny it. I'll be the first to say I'm bisexual: *(Beat)* Buy me something? I'll be sexual.

DANNY: I have a wife.

TALLULAH: And I have a Chihuahua. What's your point?

(DANNY *immediately gets up from his chair, pulls his wallet from his pocket, shows* TALLULAH *an inside picture.*

DANNY: Here.

TALLULAH: And who is this scrawny creature?

DANNY: *(Loaded)* Her name is Ruth. She's—*three.*

TALLULAH: Ohh. Baby Ruth. How sweet. You have any others in here? Almond Joy? Peppermint Patty? Peter Paul?

DANNY: *(Grabbing the picture back)* I might have known you didn't like children.

TALLULAH: On the contrary. I adore them. It's just that I was never able to—well— *(She stops mid-sentence. Beat)*

DANNY: *(Curious)* Able to—what?

TALLULAH: *Become* someone's mother. Have children. And don't you dare start feeling all sorry for me and what not. I mean, there are worse things in life than not

being able to bear a child. *(Then softer/slowly)* Not to say
I wouldn't have *relished* that opportunity: A little girl
with blonde curly locks twirling in her peach-colored
summer dress beneath the gazebo. Or a boy. Ha. Could
you imagine me—mother to some strapping young
lad whom all the young ladies would fawn over and
all the other boys would envy? *(Growing melancholic)*
Me. Tallulah. Someone's mother. *(Pause. She finishes her
drink.)* Well-well-well. Will you lookey here? My glass
appears to be empty again. Do me a favor, would you
Mr Miller? Pour me a tad more of that raccoon piss you
people call Scotch.

DANNY: Miss Bankhead, I think you've had (quite
enough)…

TALLULAH: *(Snapping)* I DON'T CARE *WHAT* YOU
FUCKING THINK! BRING ME THE GODDAMN
BOTTLE!!

(DANNY is thrown off by TALLULAH's outburst.)

TALLULAH: *(With contempt)* Please.

(DANNY reluctantly retrieves the bottle.)

TALLULAH: *(Drunk and dark)* And no more Miss
Bankhead.

(TALLULAH takes a sip as DANNY snarls.)

TALLULAH: *(Slurring a bit)* You don't like me very
much, do you, Mr Danny Miller?

DANNY: I don't dislike you if that's what you're asking.

TALLULAH: Cut the shit and answer the question.

DANNY: I don't know what you want me to say.

TALLULAH: You. Don't. Like me.

(Beat)

DANNY: Alright. No. I don't.

TALLULAH: And why, pray tell, is that?

DANNY: Does it matter?

TALLULAH: Not particularly.

DANNY: Then why ask why?

TALLULAH: Call it curiosity.

DANNY: Alright then: I—I think you're crude.

TALLULAH: Oh, come-come now. You certainly can do better than that.

DANNY: I think you will do or say anything to get attention. No matter how much it embarrasses me or humiliates yourself.

TALLULAH: Some would call that truth.

DANNY: Not me.

TALLULAH: Of course not you. Which is your *raison d'être*.

DANNY: My what?

TALLULAH: Your reason for not liking me. I frighten you. *Truth* frightens you.

DANNY: *(Redirecting)* We really should get back to work.

TALLULAH: Yes. Work. Because that's all you DO, isn't it? You sit in some dank and dreary room. Keeping yourself safely tucked away from feeling or emotion or anything that makes you feel more human.

DANNY: *(Caught/nervous/defensive)* I didn't know I was going to be psychologically examined this afternoon.

TALLULAH: And I didn't know I would stumble upon such a fascinating case study. *(Beat)* What is your story, anyhow?

DANNY: I don't have a story.

TALLULAH: Oh, we *all* got stories, baby. And I'm just curious as to what yours might be. I mean, *something* had to have given birth to that bug up your ass.

(The telephone rings again. An unnerved DANNY *dashes over and picks up the receiver.)*

DANNY: *(Angrily Into phone)* What?! *(…)* Yeah-yeah. Put it through. *(…)* Yeah. This is he. Who's this?? *(His voice immediately softens, becoming nervous and affectionate)* Oh. Hi. Umm. What's going on? Are you here already? I thought your flight was at— *(…)* What? What did you say? *(…)* You're not? *(Crestfallen)* I—I don't understand. I mean, what made you change your mind? *(…)* But I was really looking forward to-- *(…)* No. Please. Wait. Don't hang up. If it's something I said I— *(He slowly puts down the receiver. Pause)*

TALLULAH: *(Delicately with compassion)* I do believe I've been on both sides of *that* conversation.

(Silence. DANNY *is despondent.)*

TALLULAH: Dahling…perhaps you need a moment or two—

DANNY: *(Growing darker)* All I need is for you to say the goddamn line. Alright?

*(*TALLULAH *stumbles back to the stool. Her prior alcohol and cocaine use becomes more and more noticeable in her present demeanor.)*

DANNY: Steve? Let's just get this done and get out of here.

(Beep. Beep. Beep)

TALLULAH: And so Patricia, as I was telling you, that *deluded* rector has—has—oh, crap! What's he done to me again?

DANNY: He has in literal effect—

TALLULAH: He's WHAT?

DANNY: He has in literal effect closed the church to you.

TALLULAH: That makes no sense. How about I simplify it? Why don't I say "he has literally closed the church to me"?

DANNY: Because that's not the line.

TALLULAH: But—

DANNY: That's not the line!

TALLULAH: But—

DANNY: *(Loud and crazy)* THAT. IS NOT. THE LIIIIIIIIINE!!

(Beat)

TALLULAH: Are you on some sort of medication?

DANNY: No.

TALLULAH: Do you see what a life without drugs has done to you?

DANNY: Again please.

TALLULAH: Because truly you should be on some form of substance.

DANNY: And you should stop taking all prescriptions whatsoever.

TALLULAH: And you, dear boy—could use a good suppository!

(Beep. Beep. Beep)

TALLULAH: And so Patricia, as I was telling you, that—that—oh, balls. Who is it again?

DANNY: It's that deluded rector.

TALLULAH: Deluded Rector. Right.

(Beep. Beep. Beep)

TALLULAH: And so Patricia, as I was telling you, that deluded rector has—oh, he's done something very naughty…

DANNY: He's closed the church to you.

TALLULAH: Of course.

(Beep. Beep. Beep)

TALLULAH: And so Patricia, as I was telling you, that deluded rectum—

DANNY: Rec*TOR*. Rec*TOR*!

TALLULAH: That's what I said.

DANNY: No. You said rectum.

TALLULAH: Oh.

(Beep. Beep. Beep)

TALLULAH: That gives it quite a different meaning.

DANNY: You missed that one, Tallulah.

(Beep. Beep)

TALLULAH: And so Patricia, as I was—

DANNY: Too soon, Tallulah.

(Beep. Beep. Beep)

TALLULAH: Umm. Yes. Well. And so, Patricia…

DANNY: Too late, Tallulah.

TALLULAH: Too soon. Too late. I cannot pull emotion out of the blue! I am an actress not a robot! You? You're just a layman! You don't understand the creative process. I simply cannot do this the way you want me to!

DANNY: Maybe if you weren't so busy getting loaded you actually *could*!

TALLULAH: Don't you DARE get saucy with me, young man. I'll have you know I'm giving a very important party at my home this evening and if you continue this harassment, I shall be forced to un-invite you!

DANNY: I wouldn't go to a party of yours if you paid me, which from what I hear is usually the norm these days. Now again!

(Beep. Beep. Beep)

TALLULAH: *(Through gritted teeth)* And so Patricia, as I was telling you— *(exploding)* what a terrible time to tell me you can't come to my party! I mean, have you no manners? Were you brought up by a pack of wolves? Everyone knows that when someone invites you to a party, you say "why, thank you very much" even if you have absolutely no intention of attending.

DANNY: But you *didn't* invite me to a party. All you said was that you were going to UN-invite me.

TALLULAH: Which means YOU WERE ALREADY INVITED!

DANNY: That's it. I give up. I just GIVE UP!

TALLULAH:	DANNY:
You give up??	
	It's a line, lady. One. Line.
It's a drab line! And you keep making me say it over and over and over.	Any actress with the most basic of skills would know to make this work…
No actress would put up with this shit…	
	But not you. Oh no. And it's not like I'm asking for Shakespeare or Chekov…
How *dare* you speak to me this way!	
	I'm not looking for the recital of sonnets or the composing of literature…
It's disgraceful…	

your bullying and your
name calling...   And it's not even the line
                               that's the problem. It's
                               YOU! You can't hold a
                               single thought in that
                               bourbon-soaked brain of
                               yours...

TALLULAH: *(In a drug-induced rant)* I DON'T KNOW
WHAT THE HELL I'M PLAYING UP HERE!! I'm
forgetting my lines. I can't remember the fucking
props. I'm wandering up here like a goddamn zombie
because I still don't know where you want me to
walk! And I simply CANNOT sputter about this
stage crashing into scenery! Now you listen to me-- I
am supposed to go onstage for the very first time in
less than seventy-two hours and I still don't have the
slightest window into this woman's character because
the great Tennessee Williams shows up drunk at every
damn stinking rehearsal!!

*(TALLULAH comes back to reality, noticing she is still in the
sound studio and DANNY is standing before her.)*

TALLULAH: *(Softer, embarrassed)* The Coconut Grove
Playhouse. I had just finished the afternoon dress
rehearsal and ohhhh, I was brilliant. The staff and
crew were so moved by my performance they actually
had tears in their eyes when they came to pay their
compliments.
But it's half-hour now. And I'm standing on the
balcony of my dressing room having what would be
my very last cigarette before curtain. Outside I can see
this amazingly endless line of people snaking around
the entire building. All of them waiting to see me. To
see the great Tallulah Bankhead play Blanche Dubois.
He wrote it for me. Did you know that? Yes. Tennessee
Williams wrote *A Streetcar Named Desire* just for me.
Walked right up to my door and offered me the

greatest role possibly ever written. And do you know what I said to him? No thank you. I did. I said no thank you. *(Beat)* I was so scared back then. Terrified. I mean, how would it look? An aging promiscuous Southern woman who drinks too much playing an aging promiscuous Southern woman who drinks too much. It was the only time I ever gave a damn about what people thought of me. And ohh, how it cost me. Dearly. So I sat and watched Jessica Tandy become a star. Playing *my* role. Speaking *my* words. In *my* goddamn play.

But tonight? Tallulah Bankhead is back. And I'm going to show them all I was *born* to play this role. *(She hears the Stage Manager's voice in her head.)*

VOICE OVER: *(Echoing)* Places, everyone. Places for the top of Act One.

TALLULAH: I take a deep breath. The longest inhale of my life. I slip on those dainty white gloves and put that cocktail hat on my head. I pick up the valise and the slip of paper—I wait offstage right in that pearly white suit with the fluffy bodice. I glance at myself in the full length mirror. No turning back now, baby. Uppp. There's my cue:

(The lights immediately change from the soundstage to the interior of the Coconut Grove Playhouse. Tallulah is now onstage in Streetcar *as we hear thunderous applause.)*

TALLULAH: *(As Blanche)* "They told me take a street-car named Desire, and then transfer to one called Cemeteries and ride six blocks and get off at Elysian Fields!"

(Muffled laughter is heard.)

TALLULAH: I didn't know that line was funny. They must be nervous for me. It's a reflex. Breathe now. Don't let it throw you. *(As Blanche)* "I'm not accustomed to having more than one drink. Two is the limit—and three! Well, tonight I had three."

(More laughter)

TALLULAH: Dammit. What do they think is so goddamn funny? *(As Blanche)* "What's happened here? I want an explanation of what's happened here."

(The laughter grows louder.)

TALLULAH: *(Realizing)* Wait-wait-wait-wait-wait. I know what this is. You didn't come out tonight to see Tallulah Bankhead play Blanche Dubois. No. You came to see Tallulah Bankhead BE Tallulah Bankhead. You came to see failure. Ruins! Well, alright then. You faggots want fun? I'll show you fun. You want camp, fellas? I'll be more vulgar than you can bear. *(As Blanche, over the top)* "I'm looking for the Pleiades, the Seven Sisters, but these girls are not out tonight. Oh, yes they are! There they are. God bless them! All in a bunch, going home from their little bridge party"…

(The lights immediately change back to the level of the studio as the laughter slowly echoes out. TALLULAH's body is trembling. She sings the laughter out of her memory.)

TALLULAH: *(Singing)*
It's a Barnum and Bailey world,
Just as phony as it can be—
But it wouldn't be make believe
if you—
(She looks at DANNY for a moment, attempting to recognize him.) Whoever you are, I have always depended on the kindness of strangers… *(Disoriented, she makes her way toward the door as she hums the remainder of the song. She slowly exits the studio… (Singing)*
Without your love,
It's a honkytonk parade—
Without your love,
It's a melody played on a…

(A stunned DANNY *is left alone onstage as the telephone rings again and the lights fade to black.)*

END OF ACT ONE

ACT TWO

(Three hours later. 6 P M. An agitated DANNY *is picking at a half-eaten sandwich. A moment of silence passes before* STEVE *calls down to him.)*

STEVE: Any mustard down there?

*(*DANNY *takes a handful of mustard packets and throws them up at the booth.)*

STEVE: Hey. Don't take this out on me. It's not my fault we can't find her.

DANNY: You're the one who let her leave. I had to take that call from Mansky. You should have kept an eye on her.

STEVE: I should have called in sick today.

DANNY: Mansky's called five times already wondering why we haven't finished this.

STEVE: Why didn't you just tell him the truth? That she's *insane.*

DANNY: I'm not going to go bad-mouthing her to Mansky. She's got enough negative press as it is.

STEVE: Wait till the critics see this film.

DANNY: Go take another look.

STEVE: Danny. We've been searching for three hours now. Let's face it: Little Sheba just ain't coming back.

(The phone rings. DANNY *is paralyzed. It rings again.)*

STEVE: You gonna get that?

DANNY: No.

STEVE: Maybe it's Bankhead.

DANNY: Maybe it's Mansky.

STEVE: You need to find out.

DANNY: Why don't you?

STEVE: Will you get the phone already?

DANNY: What am I going to say if it's Mansky??

STEVE: Just come clean. About everything. The guy is in the movie business for Christ's sake. I'm sure he's heard it all.

DANNY: *(Calming down)* You know, you're right. Of course. I mean, maybe it's not even him. *(He lifts the receiver. (Into phone)* Hello? *(…)* Ohhh. Mr Mansky. So nice to hear from you again. *(…)* Actually? No. We didn't get it done yet. *(…)* Why?

STEVE: Oh boy.

DANNY: Well. That's a very good question. You see, we have had a few—ohh, how shall I put this—*challenges* with Miss Bankhead this afternoon—regarding her overall—*behavior.*

STEVE: Ha!

DANNY: What's wrong with her? Have you *met* her?? *(…)* Of course. And I would so very much like to do that, Sir—but—she is gone.

STEVE: Don't tell him that.

DANNY: Well. Not gone exactly. Miss Bankhead just went out for a little stroll. To get some fresh air. Alone. And now we can't seem to find her. Anywhere.

STEVE: Wrap it up, Miller.

DANNY: Well. No. We've located her Bentley and according to calls and complaints she's been stumbling into every sound stage except back into this one. *(…)* No. Not to worry: the entire lot is in lockdown. She couldn't leave here if she was armed and dangerous (which is not that far off.)

STEVE: Hang up already!

DANNY: Yes sir. Mmm-hmm. Okay. Yes. Alright. Thank you so much for calling. *(He hangs up the receiver, panics)* I'm going to lose my job.

STEVE: He didn't say that.

DANNY: He might as well have!

STEVE: Danny just calm down.

(TALLULAH enters unbeknownst to him, holding a pack of cigarettes.)

DANNY: *(Starting to lose it)* "What's wrong with her." If a psychiatrist had been in this place today? He would have ordered two straight jackets: one for her and another just in case she chewed her way out of the first!

(TALLULAH reacts.)

STEVE: *(Trying to warn him)* Umm. Danny?

DANNY: Because he's not here. He doesn't know. He can't see how much of a loony tune this woman really is.

STEVE: Danny.

DANNY: And that *voice*. When did she become so *affected??* With her dahhhhling this and her dahhhhhhling that. She sounds like a moose on a mating call.

TALLULAH: Lucky for you I don't have antlers!

(DANNY turns around, darts toward TALLULAH.)

DANNY: Where the hell have you been? We've been waiting for nearly three hours.

TALLULAH: Yes. Well. There was a *huge* line in the ladies room. *(Sniffs)* It's gone now. *(She wipes any remaining powder from her nose.)*

DANNY: Look, I just got chewed out by one of the studio heads so can we PUHLEEZE just wrap this up?

TALLULAH: Of course.

DANNY: Thank you.

TALLULAH: Just give me a moment to prepare. *(She tosses her cigarettes on the table.)*

DANNY: Steve? Are you all set?

STEVE: I would be if I had that mustard.

TALLULAH: And *SO* Patricia, as I was telling you.
And so, *PATRICIA*, as I was telling you.
And so Patricia, *AS* I was telling you.
And so Patricia, as I *WAS* telling you.
And so Patricia, as I was *TELLING* you.
And so Patricia, as I was telling *YOU*.
(Beat. To DANNY*)* Dahling, which one of those do you like best?

DANNY: *(Deflated)* I don't know.

TALLULAH: You don't have a preference?

DANNY: No.

TALLULAH: That's certainly no way to go through life.

DANNY: Alright then: I don't care.

TALLULAH: How can you not care?

DANNY: Because I don't.

TALLULAH: Why?

DANNY: Because.

TALLULAH: Because is not an answer.

DANNY: It is to me.

TALLULAH: *(Calling)* Steve, dahling?

STEVE: Yeah?

TALLULAH: Did you happen to hear me warm up just now?

STEVE: Yeah.

TALLULAH: Did you also happen to like the way I performed one line over the others?

STEVE: Yeah.

TALLULAH: And which one was that?

STEVE: The fourth.

(TALLULAH tosses DANNY a look.)

TALLULAH: Are you quite certain?

STEVE: Yeah.

TALLULAH: *(Back to DANNY)* See how easy that was? Steve can make choices. Steve can commit to decision. Steve knows what he wants.

DANNY: Well, Steve is not in charge here! I am. Now let's go!

(Beep. Beep. Beep)

TALLULAH: And so Patricia, as I was telling you—I need my purse. Where's my purse? *(Panicking)* Where's my goddamn purse?!

DANNY: *(Crossing to the purse)* I put it over here.

TALLULAH: You touched my purse?!

(DANNY hands TALLULAH the bag.)

DANNY: I just moved it.

TALLULAH: Touching a woman's purse is like touching her vagina! *(Beat)* Course, I can only fit so much in the purse. *(She takes out a prescription bottle and opens it. She pops a few pills into her mouth.)*

DANNY: *(Concerned)* What are those?

TALLULAH: *(Covering)* Breath mints.

DANNY: In a prescription bottle??

TALLULAH: Codeine happens to be leading the fight against halitosis.

DANNY: What kind of doctor would prescribe that many pills at once?

TALLULAH: I don't know. It's not my prescription.

(Beep. Beep. Beep)

TALLULAH: And so Patricia, as I was telling you, that deluded rector has—

STEVE: Cut. Dammit!

DANNY: What's wrong?

STEVE: The tape jammed.

DANNY: Well—pull it out.

TALLULAH: *(Aside)* If I had a nickel every time I said that to a man? Wait, I would *owe* money!

STEVE: Looks like we're going to need a new reel. There's one next door.

DANNY: *Nobody Move.* I'll be right back.

TALLULAH: *(Pointedly)* Actually, Steve dahling—why don't you make the run instead? This way Mr Miller and I can get better acquainted.

DANNY: That's alright. I can go.

TALLULAH: *(Demanding/stopping him)* You will stay *here!*

(Beat)

DANNY: Steve?

STEVE: Yeah.

DANNY: Go on.

TALLULAH: *(Calling)* Oh, and Steve dear? *(Looks at Danny, loaded)* Take your time.

(The light to the control room goes out as TALLULAH *retrieves her cigarettes.)*

TALLULAH: *(Seductively)* Well-well-well. Alone at last.

DANNY: Don't get any ideas.

TALLULAH: Oh, dahling, if I were hungry for a man? I would want a meal. Not an hors d'oeuvre.

DANNY: Where'd you get the cigarettes?

TALLULAH: I sold my virginity to a tobacco farmer. *(Beat)* I suppose you frown on this little vice as well.

DANNY: Actually—can I bum one?

TALLULAH: Ahh. You got potential, kid. Two points.

*(*TALLULAH *throws* DANNY *the pack. He grabs a lighter and starts to light his own cigarette while she stands holding hers.)*

TALLULAH: And such a gentleman. Don't you know how to treat a lady?

DANNY: Of course. I just don't see one here. *(He lights his cigarette in spite of her.)*

TALLULAH: *(Impressed)* Ahh. Sarcasm. Another two points. Don't make me catch up. *(A subtle threat)* You won't like the way I play.

*(*DANNY *lights* TALLULAH's *cigarette. They both awkwardly take a long inhale.)*

TALLULAH: Simply marvelous, isn't it?

DANNY: What is?

TALLULAH: That very first inhale. That initial draft one pulls deep into the lungs. That sliver of a second when the mind—clears. A clean slate. Not a worry in the world.

DANNY: I never thought of it that way.

TALLULAH: That's why we can't seem to give it up, you see. We need that first hit to cleanse away all the sins we've committed since our last smoke. It's a baptism of sorts, really. *(Indicates cigarette)* And this? This little stick is my Eucharist.

DANNY: You have a very blasphemous way of looking at things.

TALLULAH: Said the sinner to the heretic.

(A loaded moment passes between TALLULAH and DANNY.)

TALLULAH: Why do you suppose the most harmful things in life give us the most pleasure?

DANNY: Like?

TALLULAH: Booze. Drugs. Sex.

DANNY: Sex? Since when is that harmful?

TALLULAH: Hell, it nearly killed me. When I first moved to Hollywood? I had just one thing on my mind.

DANNY: To become a star?

TALLULAH: To fuck Gary Cooper. And I did too. But he was DUH-READFUL in bed. Horrible. I've had vaccination shots that stayed inside me longer. And as if that weren't enough, the son-of-a-bitch gave me a little reminder of our encounter. Gonorrhea. I nearly died from it. Had to have an emergency hysterectomy. At only thirty-one years old. *(Beat)* That's why I could never have— *(Beat)* Well. *(Beat)* What the hell difference does it make now, hmm?

DANNY: And yet that didn't stop you from—

TALLULAH:—whoring around?

DANNY: I didn't say that.

TALLULAH: You didn't have to.

(Beat)

DANNY: You can't stop, can you?

TALLULAH: What?

DANNY: The drinking, the pills.

TALLULAH: *(With simple honesty)* No. I can't. And so fucking what? *Everyone* has their vices. Mine just all come out to play at the same time.

DANNY: Which keeps you from living in reality.

TALLULAH: You wouldn't know reality if it bit you in the ass. *(Beat)* I woke up. A few weeks back. Dove into the pool and started my laps. Back and forth. Breaststroke. Sidestroke. Backstroke. Like I do every morning or afternoon or whenever the fuck I choose to wake up. Anyhoo, after a hundred or so paddles, I feel this pain in my chest. This, this—piercing. And then suddenly—suddenly I—I find myself having trouble catching my breath. So. I crawl out of the water. Dry myself off. Pour myself a cocktail. Pop a few pills. And then fall dead asleep. *(Beat)* But when I wake up? The pain. The labored breathing—well—still there. And no matter how much I drink or smoke or snort—this pain—this—*thing*—it refuses to leave me alone. *(Beat)* Emphysema. *(Beat)* Six months. That's what they give me. Six fucking months.

(DANNY is stunned.)

DANNY: Tallulah—

TALLULAH: Ehhh, I'm hardly afraid of dying. I just don't want to be there when it happens.

DANNY: Oh, my God. I am so—

TALLULAH: What? Sorry? Bullshit. How can one possibly feel sorrow for a person one doesn't like? Oh, but I forgot. You of course can. Being of that *nature.*

DANNY: What are you talking about?

TALLULAH: Deception.

DANNY: Just because I said I'm sorry you're d— *(He stops.)*

TALLULAH: Go on, Say it. Dying. Yes. I am. But let me tell you something, buster. I would rather spend an eternity of dying than a lifetime of dead. Like you.

DANNY: *(Defensive)* Like me? How like me? I'm not dead.

TALLULAH: Then what precisely do you call this? Because quite frankly, when I look at you? I don't see anything there. Oh, I can make out a body and hear a voice. But there's nothing—*there.*

DANNY: I am going to find Steve.

TALLULAH: See, you can't possibly convince me for one moment that THIS is what you dreamed about becoming.

DANNY: Steve?

TALLULAH: That HERE is where you pictured yourself working.

DANNY: Steve.

TALLULAH: That NOW is the time you THOUGHT you'd be having.

DANNY: Steve!

TALLULAH: I WANT TO KNOW WHY!

STEVE: *(Over speaker)* You looking for me?

DANNY: *(Flustered)* Steve. Good. I mean. We're ready to start again.

STEVE: Great.

DANNY: *(To* TALLULAH*)* You all set?

TALLULAH: Of course, darling. *(Then in a cryptic whisper)* Let the games begin.

*(*DANNY *understands her meaning as he signals to* STEVE.*)*

(Beep. Beep. Beep)

TALLULAH: And so Patricia, as I was telling you— *(Deliberately)* —hmm. So sorry. My mind seems to have gone blank. Completely blank.

DANNY: *(In an angry whisper)* Don't think I don't know what you're doing.

TALLULAH: Why, Daniel, what*ever* do you mean?

DANNY: Stop.

TALLULAH: Surrender.

DANNY: No.

TALLULAH: *(To Steve)* Again! *(A soft-spoken backhand to* DANNY*)* I told you wouldn't like the way I play. Because I—very much like you—*cheat*.

(Beep. Beep. Beep)

TALLULAH: And so Patricia, as I was telling you— ohhhh, my-my-my. I'm afraid this may take a bit of time.

DANNY: *(Surrendering)* Steve?

STEVE: Yeah.

DANNY: It looks like we're gonna need a little more time down here to, to, to—

STEVE:—rehearse?

DANNY: Yeah. Rehearse.

TALLULAH: Steve dahling?

STEVE: Yeah.

TALLULAH: I think what Daniel's asking, is that you give us a tad more space. *(Demanding)* Alone.

STEVE: I'll wait outside.

(A door is heard closing: Beat and then:)

DANNY: *(On the verge)* What do you want?

TALLULAH: Ohh, don't play games with me, young man. I'm too old. Too tired. And tragically now too sober. But thankfully the latter can change.

(TALLULAH finds the bottle and pours two glasses. She attempts to hand one to DANNY who refuses.)

TALLULAH: Suit yourself. *(She drinks her cocktail. Then his.)* Now then. You can tell me. And you want to know why you can tell me? Because I'm the only person you *can* tell. Sometimes, my dearest—we can say things to strangers we wouldn't dream of confiding in our very best of friends. I won't judge. Christ, how the hell could I? And don't worry. I'll take it to my grave (which according to those bastard doctors should be any moment now). So. Danny. Tell me.

(DANNY starts to walk away from TALLULAH:)

TALLULAH: Who was he?

(DANNY stops. Trapped, caught. Pause)

DANNY: *(With difficulty)* Just a guy.

TALLULAH: Do you think you could elaborate a tad?

(Beat and then:)

DANNY: College… We met our sophomore year at college. He used to sit two seats in front of me. Well. Not really in front of me. More like diagonally across from me. And to the left. Or was I to the left? No. He was behind me and I sat in front of him but to the right of—

TALLULAH: Jesus Christ! Did I not just say I have six months to live? Get to the goddamn visual!

DANNY: The what?

TALLULAH: The visual. Baby. What did he look like?

DANNY: Okay. Umm. The visual. Lets see. Umm. Average height. Umm. Real solid looking guy. Brownish hair. Oh. And teeth. He had teeth.

TALLULAH: Good.

DANNY: I mean. A. Umm. Really cool smile. Handsome in a not-so-handsome way. But you need to know I had a girlfriend at the time.

TALLULAH: Nothing wrong with a little subplot.

(DANNY shoots TALLULAH a look.)

TALLULAH: Proceed.

DANNY: There was this, umm—drive-in theatre where we used to hang out on weekends. We would never go in or anything like that. We used to just drive on this dirt road behind the lot in Eddie's truck. Until we found just the right spot—you know, so we could still see the screen through the trees? Anyway. We could never hear the actual audio track cause we didn't have any speakers. So we used to create our own dialogue instead. Making up our own lines and stuff. *(laughs to himself)* I mean, just crazy talk. Like things that had nothing to do with the real story. *(His laughter turns serious.)* It's as if pretending to be all these different characters allowed us to speak words to each other that—well—that we could never really say in life.

TALLULAH: The magic of the movies.

DANNY: *(Dismissing)* Yeah. Well.

(Beat)

TALLULAH: *(Delicately)* This, umm —

DANNY: Eddie.

TALLULAH: Eddie. Yes. Did you love him?

DANNY: *(Instinctively)* No. *(Then)* I—I don't know. I— *(Then admitting softly)* —yes.

TALLULAH: And did you— *(She gestures)*

DANNY: Huh?

TALLULAH: Did you— *(She mumbles)*

DANNY: What?

TALLULAH: Don't make me spell this shit out.

DANNY: *(Embarrassed)* Oh. Umm. Yeah.

*(*TALLULAH *rolls her eyes. Then:)*

TALLULAH: So why did it end?

DANNY: Because I had an obligation.

TALLULAH: To the man you were in love with or to the woman who loved you?

DANNY: To our unborn child.

TALLULAH: I see. Well. That is not a little subplot.

DANNY: She went and got herself pregnant.

TALLULAH: She got *herself* pregnant? Now THAT is a conception I'd like to see!

DANNY: I was going to be a father. And I had to do the right thing. So we got married. That was that. End of story.

TALLULAH: No-no-no-no-no, dahling. I don't think so.

DANNY: You wanted to know what happened so I told you.

TALLULAH: Not everything you didn't.

DANNY: I did.

TALLULAH: Your daughter. Remember her? Dear Baby Ruth.

DANNY: She doesn't have anything to do with this.

TALLULAH: You even showed me a picture. She's three. That's what you told me: she's three.

DANNY: So what?

TALLULAH: *(Overlapping)* How could that possibly be true? Not if that wife of yours gave birth to her in college.

DANNY: Would you just stop?

TALLULAH: *(Overlapping)* She would certainly be much older than that by now.

DANNY: I mean it. Enough already!

TALLULAH: *(Overlapping)* But then why would you be carrying a picture of her at only three years old?

DANNY: Shut up!

TALLULAH: What happened to your daughter?

DANNY: Nothing.

TALLULAH: Where is she now?

DANNY: At home.

TALLULAH: Where is she, dammit?!

DANNY: I don't know!

TALLULAH: WHERE IS SHE?!

DANNY: GONE! ALRIGHT?! YOU FUCKING BITCH?! MY DAUGHTER IS GONE!

(TALLULAH is shaken from DANNY's outburst. Beat)

TALLULAH: Gone. Where?

(DANNY is stuck.)

TALLULAH: *(Supportive)* Truth. Danny.

(DANNY *takes a moment. Then:*)

DANNY: *(Difficult and slowly)* We got married. She had the baby. A girl. Ruth. So what could I do? I stopped seeing him. Then started again. Then stopped. I couldn't leave her—and I sure as hell didn't want to leave him. So. There I was. Right smack in the middle of Responsibility and Desire. You ever been there?

TALLULAH: Too many times, baby.

DANNY: She confronts me. Again and again. Until finally I can't lie anymore and simply tell her the truth: that I am in love with someone who has never been and never will be—*her. (Beat)* She goes totally insane with revenge. Makes me pack up my things and move out of the house. And throughout it all? I don't break down. She files for divorce. I sign half of all the nothing I have over to her. And I don't break down. I—*stand* there. In that courtroom. Labeled by them as this sexual deviant. As I watch that judge sign away my right to ever see my daughter's face again. And throughout it all? I do not break down. Not once do I br— *(He finally does break down, sobbing uncontrollably.)*

TALLULAH: That's it dahling. Let it all out now.

(DANNY sobs louder as TALLULAH becomes unnerved.)

TALLULAH: Alright. Alright, dear.

(DANNY continues crying. Another burst of sobs)

TALLULAH: That's enough now.

(DANNY continues sobbing.)

TALLULAH: *(Under her breath)* Oh shit. *(She quickly searches her purse, looking for anything that will make him feel better. She pulls out a set of keys and jingles them.)*

TALLULAH: *(As if talking to a child)* Look. Keys. I have keys!

(DANNY continues crying.)

TALLULAH: *(Now as if talking to a dog)* A walk! Who wants to go for a walk? Come on Boy. Come on now. Come—

(DANNY is still inconsolable as TALLULAH remains at a loss. Not knowing what else to do, she takes a seat beside him and simply places her hand upon his.)

TALLULAH: Ugh. I'm exhausted.

DANNY: *(Humbly and genuine)* I. umm. *Lied* to you earlier. About my daughter. She's not three. She turned eighteen about a month ago. So I decided to finally get in touch with her. You know. Now that I *could*? *(Beat)* She was actually happy to hear from me. She even wanted to meet. So I sent her a ticket. *(Beat)* I don't even know what she looks like. *(Beat)* She was supposed to fly out this afternoon. *(Beat)* She's not coming. Changed her mind I guess. And I don't blame her for not ever wanting to see me again.

TALLULAH: She doesn't want to see you *today*. You don't know what's going on in that girl's head. Listen. Sweetie. You mustn't discredit the marvelous thing you did. *You opened a door*. Whether your daughter steps in or not is out of your hands.

DANNY: I never should have left. She needed a father. I should have stayed and made it work.

TALLULAH: Why? So you could be more miserable than you already are? Ohh, baby—we are not so different after all. You and me. I did the same thing my entire life that you're doing right now. I blamed myself. I carried a burden of guilt with me for years until one day I realized—it was never mine to cart. You see, my mama died of blood poisoning just three weeks after giving birth. To me. Yes. In fact. I was christened right beside her open casket. Hell of a way to start one's life, hmm?

And Daddy? He took to the bottle soon afterwards. Ohh. How that man resented me. Blamed me. Blamed me for taking away his beautiful bride. And before long? I blamed me.

So I actually *became* the sinner Daddy told me I was. Had my first cigarette when I was nine. Was drinking by the time I was twelve. The drugs. The sex. The whole lot of it. All done in an effort to ease the pain. Until that *becomes* the pain. And by the time I figure all this shit out? I'm a sixty-three year old woman six months away from death.

Set yourself free, Danny boy. If nothing else you need, no, you MUST live the life you want to live.

(Beat)

DANNY: I—I can't.

TALLULAH: Then boo-fucking-hoo. You little shit.

DANNY: Ohh, open your eyes! You have no idea what I would be up against.

TALLULAH: Don't I?

DANNY: People just don't accept that kind of thing in this day and age.

TALLULAH: People are stupid. Calculatingly cruel. There's always going to be someone who doesn't like the way you dress or the way you act or the way you think and who gives a flying fuck?? Why should you live YOUR life by THEIR rules?

DANNY: You're hardly one to lecture me. You don't exactly have the best track record when it comes to relationships.

TALLULAH: Because I didn't want to be tied down. I used men like they used me. No harm. No foul.

DANNY: What about love?

TALLULAH: Over-rated. I'd much rather be in lust than in love.

DANNY: Even if it means dying alone?

TALLULAH: We ALL die alone, baby. You ever read an obituary that suggested otherwise?

DANNY: You know what I mean.

TALLULAH: Listen here, when I strike out at something like love? I keep my cleats on. Step right back up to the plate. I may not hit a home run but at least I let a stranger get to second or third.

DANNY: Well, I can't do that. I wasn't brought up that way.

TALLULAH: Ha. You are looking at the daughter of a Congressman and Speaker of the House. The granddaughter of a United States Senator. No one had a better upbringing than me. And just look how deliciously disgraceful I turned out.

DANNY: You have no respect for anything.

TALLULAH: Baby, if I had my life to live over again? I'd make the same damn mistakes. Only sooner.

DANNY: Does that include your career?

TALLULAH: *(Redirecting)* We really must get back to work.

DANNY: Answer the question.

TALLULAH: *(Calling)* Steve? Dahling, are you up there?

DANNY: Bad move. Already played. Now come on: if you had to do it all over again? You can't possibly tell me you'd do it exactly the same way?

TALLULAH: I'm telling you I don't wish to discuss it.

DANNY: So you *do* have regrets.

TALLULAH: I regret everything. But repent for nothing.

DANNY: Sounds like a big bag of bullshit if you ask me.

TALLULAH: I didn't ask you.

DANNY: Come on. I told you *why*. Now you tell me *how*. HOW does someone go from being on the top of the world to the bottom of the barrel in the blink of an eye?

TALLULAH: I don't believe I care for your tone.

DANNY: Of course you don't. For what I am suggesting would involve living in reality. Something you and your cigarettes and your suitcases full of functioning narcotics would know nothing about!

TALLULAH: I HAPPEN TO BE FAMOUS!

DANNY: Yes, but for what? Swearing like a sailor? Greeting your guests at the door stark naked?

TALLULAH: Yes. That's me. That is Tallulah!

DANNY: And you're proud of that??

TALLULAH: What I am proud of, dahling, is that I have always lived my life as Tallulah Bankhead. The rebel. The heretic. The woman who was bold enough to tell people the way it was even though she was demonized for every word!

DANNY: And sabotaged her career in the process!

(TALLULAH *is clearly shaken.*)

TALLULAH: *(Indignant)* Listen, Buster. I played Jezebel!

DANNY: Which during rehearsals you had to be taken out in an ambulance due to infections from your promiscuity!

TALLULAH: Sabina in *Skin of Our Teeth*. Three hundred and fifty-nine performances!

DANNY: Too bad the entire cast would show up five minutes before curtain in order to save themselves from your outrageous tantrums!

TALLULAH: *(Proudly) The Little Foxes.*

DANNY: Lillian Hellman stopped speaking to you twenty years ago!

TALLULAH: I was brilliant in *Lifeboat!*

DANNY: Yes. You were. Damn shame you were so hated by then Hollywood wouldn't even nominate you for an Oscar. And don't even get me started on *Streetcar*—or as Tennessee Williams put it—the first time a drag queen ever played Blanche Dubois!

TALLULAH: Tenny is a drunk! That 'ol sister doesn't knows what she's saying half the time! It was the others. All those manicured men. The theatre queens who claimed to have discovered Tallulah but then ripped her limb from bloody limb!

DANNY: You have no one to blame for that but yourself.

TALLULAH: At least I had the balls to be who I was instead of taking some hostage of a wife in order to prove some ridiculous lie to whomever was bored enough to care!

DANNY: No. You just fucked everyone instead. And it didn't matter who or where or how—as long as you didn't have to be alone with yourself and see exactly who you really were!

TALLULAH: At least I BECAME someone. I DID something with my life. Unlike you. Poor little boy. Alright. I may have fucked up my own life! But just MY LIFE. You took down four including your own!!

(DANNY is stung. Long pause)

DANNY: *(Slowly and with increasing passion)* This film is your last picture. And you want to know what? It stinks. You see, I've been editing this piece of trash for the past three months. And I've watched it over and over and over. And I've cut and cut and cut with the sole purpose of making you look better. Yes. You. The great Talullah Bankhead. Oh, you remember her, don't you? She's the actress who can't remember her lines. Or makes up her own lines. Or says another character's lines instead of her own. Or better yet, she simply says nothing because she thinks she doesn't have a line when she actually does. Which ironically is the best part of this picture because you're—not—speaking. And it's me, me who has to make you look good. Cutting and snipping and pasting so the whole world will be fooled into thinking that Tallulah Bankhead is still the greatest actress who's ever graced the silver screen. But it's all a lie. One big goddamn lie. So let's not bullshit each other. Because we both damn well know the truth. *(Beat)* You stopped being an actress *years* ago to become—*a celebrity*. And now? You're washed up. *(Beat)* You're a has-been. And a fraud.

(Pause. Then calmly and confidently, holding herself together:)

TALLULAH: My dear boy. I must warn you for your own sake: this attempt of yours to humiliate me is amateurish compared to my own lifelong degradation. No one can hurt me more than I have hurt myself. So if you think you can disgrace me with anything you say? Get your candy ass in line. Because it's already been done. *By. Me.* So I'm afraid you're just wasting my time.

DANNY: And you, lady, are wasting mine.

STEVE: *(Over speaker)* And I'm still on the clock here.

TALLULAH: *(Touched and sincerely apologetic)* Oh Steve dahling. Of course. I believe, I'm quite ready.

DANNY: So am I.

STEVE: Great.

DANNY: *(To* TALLULAH*)* Do you need the line again?

TALLULAH: Steve, dear: please tell Mr Miller I do not require his assistance.

STEVE: Danny, Miss Bankhead says that she —

DANNY: Umm. I can hear her.

STEVE: Sorry.

DANNY: Let's just get this over with.

(Beep. Beep. Beep)

TALLULAH: And so Patricia, as I was telling you, that *deluded* rector has in literal effect closed the church to me.

STEVE: Shit.

DANNY: What?

STEVE: I forgot to hit the record button.

TALLULAH: That's alright, Steve dahling. I'm a professional. Let's just go again, shall we?

DANNY: Fine. You ready this time?

STEVE: Yes. I am.

(Beep. Beep. Beep)

TALLULAH: And so Patricia, as I was telling you, that *deluded* rector has in literal effect closed the church to me.

DANNY: Steve?

STEVE: It's good.

TALLULAH: I can do better.

DANNY: But, we don't need —

TALLULAH: I said I can do better.

DANNY: Fine.

(Beep. Beep. Beep)

TALLULAH: And so Patricia, as I was telling you, that *deluded* rector has in literal effect closed the church to me.

DANNY: Steve?

STEVE: Damn.

DANNY: What?

STEVE: That *was* better.

TALLULAH: Lovely. Now then gentlemen, if there's nothing further, I believe it's time I take my leave.

DANNY: Wait a minute. Why didn't you just say the line that way in the first place?

TALLULAH: *(Affectionately)* Because if I did, dahling— we wouldn't have gotten to know each other now, would we? Besides, neither one of us is in a big hurry to go anywhere.

STEVE: *(Clears throat)* Actually, I am. I promised my kids I'd take them to the Dodger game and Kofax is pitching. Can I leave? Please.

DANNY: Sure. We're all finished here.

STEVE: See ya Danny. Goodnight. Miss Bank—

(TALLULAH gives STEVE a look.)

STEVE: Goodnight, Tallulah.

TALLULAH: Take care, Steve dahling.

(The lights to the control room turn off. Pause)

DANNY: I—umm—saw—you in *Streetcar* at the Coconut Grove Playhouse. And—I—saw *The Little Foxes*. And I snuck into the premieres of *Stage Door Canteen* and *Lifeboat*. In fact, I, ummm—saw you in practically everything you have ever done. How I used to watch you. I would actually tremble when I left the theatre. Because you were so—extraordinary.

Why did you piss all over that production of *Streetcar*?
You deliberately gave a bad performance. Throwing
lines out to the audience. Camping it up for your
fans. You know that's not the way that role should be
played.

TALLULAH: Yes, dahling—but I also know that's what
they all wanted to see. Show business, baby. We
always give the people what they want.

DANNY: Suppose you didn't have to, anymore.

TALLULAH: Hmm?

DANNY: Show me.

TALLULAH: What?

DANNY: Your Blanche Dubois.

TALLULAH: Darling, I haven't played that part (in
years)…

DANNY: Show me. Tallulah. Please. I promise I won't
laugh at you.

(TALLULAH *takes a moment, not knowing whether to trust*
DANNY *or not. When she finally decides to do this, she gives
the best performance of her career.*)

TALLULAH: *(As Blanche)* "This man is a gentleman and
he respects me. What he wants is my companionship.
Having great wealth sometimes makes people lonely.
A cultivated woman, a woman of intelligence and
breeding, can enrich a man's life—immeasurably.
I have those things to offer, and time doesn't take
them away. Physical beauty is passing. A transitory
possession. But beauty of the mind and richness of the
spirit and tenderness of the heart—and I have all of
those things—aren't taken away, but grow! Increase
with the years! How strange I should be called a
destitute woman! When I have all these treasures

locked in my heart. *[a choked sob comes from her]* I think of myself—as a very very rich woman!"

(Pause)

DANNY: *(Deeply moved)* Tallulah. I'm sorry.

TALLULAH: No you're not.

DANNY: Would you just let me apologize here?

TALLULAH: No, I won't. You said what you had to say and despite the brutality of it, I respect your honesty. *(A painful admission)* You were right about everything you said. *(She starts for the door.)*

DANNY: *(With difficulty)* I—I—

TALLULAH: What baby?

DANNY: Nothing. Everything. I've missed so much.

TALLULAH: Then do something about it. Take a trip. Take a drink. Take a lover. Anything. At least make a choice. Choose something other than this life that you've created for yourself. *You don't have to be this unhappy.* There is always going to be pain in life, baby. But suffering? That one is optional. *(She goes to leave again.)*

DANNY: I thought I was invited to your party tonight?

TALLULAH: Yes. And then I un-invited you.

DANNY: Well. I'd like to be re-invited.

(TALLULAH is touched. She moves closer to DANNY, placing the palm of her hand on his face.)

TALLULAH: My dear, sweet boy. There is no party. Hasn't been one for some time. People just don't come around like they used to.

DANNY: I could. Tonight maybe. Now even.

TALLULAH: Spare me your pity.

DANNY: Only if you spare me yours. Come on. What do you say? A quick drink wouldn't exactly kill me.

TALLULAH: Honey, the way I pour? Don't be so sure. *(She heads for the door.)*

DANNY: So it's a date?

TALLULAH: *(Nods)* Mmmm. And apparently another sexless night.

(TALLULAH exits the studio. DANNY laughs to himself, grabs his coat and exits as the lights fade to black.)

END OF PLAY